The Dating Game

How To Find Yourself While Looking For Mr. Right Title

Shawnda Patterson

For booking and other business

related inquiries please visit

www.bronzegoddess01.com

"Be with the guy that ruins your lipstick, not your mascara."

-Unknown

THE DATING GAME

DEDICATION

THE DATING GAME

From America Street to the American dream. You taught me how to dream big. This book is dedicated to Clifford Whitfield, the first man who ever loved me. I love you Daddy! May you rest in peace. This book is also dedicated to the only two people in the world who knew I was writing it, my husband and my sister. You two are my biggest cheerleaders. My only hope is that I can be half as good to you two as you both have been to me.

CONTENTS

THE DATING GAME

ABOUT THE AUTHOR

THE DATING GAME

I was born in Charleston, South Carolina in 1978 to a Southern belle and a preacher. My mother taught me how to be ladylike and carry myself with class. My father taught me that men can't be altered at the altar and the importance of being whole before entering a relationship. The beliefs and values instilled in me by my parents never left me. After high school I joined the United States Army and later pursued my dream of becoming a classically trained chef by studying at the International Culinary School at the Art Institute of Atlanta. On October 9, 2004, in my father's living room I married the love of my life. My father presided over our intimate four-person ceremony. We are now the proud parents of three beautiful daughters and reside in Atlanta, Georgia.

As a hobby, I began making makeup and hair tutorials on YouTube, but I always felt I had so much more to offer. At the time I could not figure out what that was. I had a forty-five minute commute to culinary school so I started listening to the Steve Harvey Morning Show. I used to look forward to hearing Steve and Shirley Strawberry's relationship advice to the letters people wrote to them. One day I received a letter from one of my YouTube viewers asking for my advice about her cheating husband. In homage to the strawberry letters I loved so much I called the video, "Strawberry Letter: Ask the Goddess." I never intended to do any additional letters but the response was overwhelming.

My inbox begun to overflow with letters from women unhappy with the course of their relationships. Although each situation is different, I quickly noticed a pattern with the women who were writing to me. Women of all ages, races, and economic backgrounds did not know their worth. As a result, they ended up in unfulfilling relationships that were not meeting their needs. After over four years and over one hundred love and relationship advice videos, I felt like someone needed to tell these women what to do before entering the dating arena. Someone needed to tell them to make sure he is worthy of you before falling head over heels for him. Someone needed to ask them whether he has just minor flaws or if there are deal breakers. Someone needed to teach them the importance of knowing your worth. That someone was me. For years I have used my YouTube channel, Bronzegoddess01, as a platform to inspire and uplift my viewers with my motivational speaking and relationship advice videos. I also began mentoring individuals one on one as an adviser. My online platform has grown tremendously, currently over 60,000 subscribers and 7.4 million views. Testimonials from women who have discovered their worth and begun to demand what they deserve in their relationships fueled my passion to write this book.

THE DATING GAME

INTRODUCTION

THE DATING GAME

Are you in a long term relationship that is not going anywhere? Do you ever ask yourself if you are even dateable? In this book you will learn, among other things, how to determine the true intentions of your love interest. You will learn how to master the art of dating and also discover ways to make yourself the ultimate catch to any man. I wrote this book for all of the amazing women out there wasting the prime of their lives on relationships that are not giving them what they want – and never will.

Whether you are a first time dater, newly divorced, or in a relationship that is going nowhere, this book was written with you in mind. Each chapter provides practical tips and advice on dating. This book will answer some of the most commonly asked questions, such as: "How do I know if he is into me," "Am I dateable," "How do I flirt," and more. Are you ready to find some answers? On to chapter one.

CHAPTER 1
KNOW YOUR WORTH/CONFIDENCE

THE DATING GAME

Know your worth! Many love and relationship therapists, counselors and experts have said this time and time again. By now you are probably sick and tired of hearing it, but that does not make it any less important. If you do not know your worth, most likely someone else will determine your worth and they will underestimate your value. Far too many people are in relationships all alone. One-sided relationships are the worst kind. So why do we stay in relationships that are no longer fulfilling our needs?

I recently received a letter from a woman who said she had been casually dating her male best friend. The friend put their relationship on hold because he wanted to pursue a relationship with another woman. He told her if things did not work out with the other woman that he would like to pick up where they had left off. Without the slightest hesitation she agreed. I must admit that I was flabbergasted when I read this. Some readers may be thinking 'well at least he was upfront and honest with her.' Maybe he was, but why did the writer eagerly agree to these preposterous conditions? Why did she not believe that she deserved better? If Instagram is good for anything it is amazing for a good quote. Here is one I love, "Know your worth. It makes no sense to be second in someone's life, when you know you're good enough to be first in someone else's."

THE DATING GAME

The love interest in the letter came back after trying to make it work with the other woman. Not surprisingly, it did not take long for him to begin cheating on the writer of the letter. Why is that? Because she gave him an opportunity to date someone else and he came back to her, right? Wrong. The writer set the tone for the relationship. She sent a very clear message by her actions that she did not think she deserved to be his first – and only – choice. Never lose who you are to please someone else. Never allow someone to treat you like you are not good enough for them. If you do not get anything else from this book, at least know that you *are* enough. You are no man's consolation prize.

You are the ultimate catch, and any man who does not know that is a fool. Unfortunately, like so many women, the writer of this letter had begun to settle. Women settle for so many reasons, like these: "we already have a child together," "being with him is better than being alone," "at least he wants to marry me," "we have already been intimate," "we have been together so long I would not even know how to start over," and so on. Women go on and on with excuses for not deserving better. This all stems from low self-esteem and a poor self-image. What causes a woman to see herself in such a negative way? Several factors affect an individual's perceptions of themselves. Some people grow up hearing negative comments from a parental or authority figure. Others may have been bullied, traumatized, were rarely complimented, or were neglected in some way. Identifying someone with a poor self-image is very easy. For one thing, they do not typically take compliments very well. If you say to them "I absolutely love that dress on you," they may say something like, "you really think so" or "I think it makes me look fat but thanks anyway." Individuals with low self-esteem also speak with a negative self-talk. They are often saying, "I could not possibly do that," "that kind of thing never happens to someone like me" or "I can't." This way of thinking manifests itself in their relationships in the form of neediness, insecurities, and of course settling. This type of individual feels lucky just to have someone, and they often involve themselves as a third party in an already-existing relationship. Before you can pursue a relationship with anyone else you must understand your own value and worth.

Your relationship status does not determine your value or your worth. Take this analogy, for example. Imagine that you have a $20 bill. What is the value of that bill? $20, right? Well, what if you take that crisp $20 bill and ball it up and throw it on the ground. What is it worth now? Still $20, right? That is a great metaphor for life. Sometimes life, and past relationships, crumbles us up and throws us on the ground. Do we no longer have value? Of course we do. Again: your relationship status does not determine your value or your worth. And mistakes from your past do not define who you will be in the future. It does not matter if you were a teen mom, are a divorcee, or are a woman with a promiscuous past. You still deserve the fulfilling and monogamous relationship you have always dreamed of. So never let your past hold you prisoner, or allow fear to creep into your thoughts.

Learn to ignore that little voice in your head telling you 'you do not deserve him' or 'you will never be happy.' These types of thoughts were born out of fear. In the book *Feel the Fear and Do It Anyway* author Susan Jeffers explains that one of the keys to overcoming fear is convincing yourself that you can handle whatever may come in any relationship or situation. The belief that you can handle anything life brings you will do wonders for your self-confidence. Jeffers suggests writing out a sign that simply states 'I will handle it.' This is what you will tell yourself whenever you are facing a challenging and new situation, such as; asking your boss for a promotion, going back to school, or even entering a new relationship. Remind yourself that just like sharks were born already knowing how to swim; you, too, were born with the skills you need to survive. In life there are many risks, but building your confidence requires that you feel the fear and do it anyway.

Dating is one of life's biggest risks-versus-rewards situations. It takes courage and confidence to get out there, meet new people, and allow yourself to be vulnerable. But to successfully do so, you must eliminate what motivational speaker Zig Ziegler calls 'stinkin thinkin.' It may be necessary to hit the reset button on the way you see yourself. Whether we are talking about the bedroom or the boardroom, self-confidence is vitally important. You are not ready to be in a healthy relationship with someone else until you can have a healthy relationship with yourself. Others often see us as we see ourselves. It is all a matter of confidence.

This section will help you determine your existing level of self-confidence. Are you going into relationships feeling that you have plenty to bring to the table, and that any man would be lucky to have you? Before answering, let's take a quick confidence quiz:

1. **I feel great about where I am in my life right now.**

    A. Always
    B. For The Most Part
    C. Rarely
    D. Never

2. **I genuinely believe that if I apply myself to any goal it is possible to achieve it.**

    A. Always
    B. For The Most Part
    C. Rarely
    D. Never

3. **When faced with adversity, I feel like there is no hope.**

    A. Never
    B. Sometimes
    C. Almost Always
    D. Always

4. **When someone breaks a promise to you, you are...**

    A. Never too disappointed. Assume they tried their best.
    B. Slightly disappointed but what is done is done.
    C. Disappointed.
    D. Very disappointed and take it personally. You can never count on people when you need them.

5. **You reward yourself for accomplishing your goals,**

    A. Always
    B. Almost Always
    C. Sometimes
    D. Never

6. **When complimented on your appearance you...**

    A. Smile and say thank you because you know you look fabulous
    B. Thank them whether you agree or not
    C. Think they are just trying to be nice but doubt their sincerity
    D. Know that they are lying because you hate the way you look

7. **You have been asked out by a guy that you find very attractive and you think...**

    A. It is about time
    B. We would make a cute couple
    C. He is out of my league
    D. He must be blind

8. **You are out with the girls and the waitress brings over a drink. She says it is from the**

gentleman at the bar. He is David Beckham, Idris Elba, and Brad Pitt fine! You think...

    A. Of course it is for me!
    B. It could be for any of us
    C. I doubt it is for me
    D. No way in the world that it is for me

9. **How do you feel about your weight?**

    A. I look good at any weight
    B. No exactly where I want to be but I still look good
    C. If I lose some weight I will look much better
    D. Nothing looks good on me no matter what I wear

10. **You are out on a date with a new guy and he claims he forgot his wallet. You think...**

    A. I will pay for dinner this time, but he better not make this mistake again.
    B. There is nothing wrong with going Dutch every now and then or taking turns paying for dates.

    C. I do not mind paying for the dates as long as he is still interested in going out.

    D. Somehow I always end up paying for things when I am with a man.

11. **A man you have been interested in for a while starts up a conversation with you. He tells you he is in a relationship but it is not going well. He says most likely they are going to break up. He asks you to dinner. You...**

    A. Tell him to give you a call once he has ended his relationship with his girlfriend

    B. Make it clear to him that friendship is all you are willing to give him

    C. Agree to dinner

    D. Agree to dinner and pursue a relationship with him. He said he was not happy, and if he is going to break up with his girlfriend anyway, what is the big deal?

If you answered mostly A's to these questions you are an ego maniac. Just kidding! You feel good about yourself and the way others see you. You are not afraid to speak your mind. You are goal oriented, confident, and believe you can achieve anything you put your mind to. You know who you are and what you bring to the table. If you answered mostly B or a combination of A and B, you are also a confident individual. And you are comfortable in your own skin. If you answered mostly Cs and Ds to these questions, you struggle with your self-image. Most likely you feel like you will not be successful in any area of your life, neither personally or professionally. There are two things you can never have too much of, and those things are shoes and confidence. So, regardless of your score results we could always build on our self-confidence (and buy more shoes while we are at it!). One could be perfectly confident in one area of life and lack confidence in another. Now that we have identified where you are let's build from there.

CHAPTER 2
ARE YOU DATEABLE? IS HE DATEABLE?

THE DATING GAME

Well, are you dateable? Before you answer that question, allow me to pose another. Do you know what you want? Every woman should have some 'must haves.' These are the nonnegotiable set-in-stone relationship basics. For example: he must be a Christian, he must live on his own, he must have ambition, and so on. Every woman's 'must have' requirements are different. One woman may not consider dating a man with a child, but she would date a man who lives with his parents.

Overall though, there are certain core issues that you should not have to sacrifice. What you compromise to get you must also compromise to keep. When you begin to lower your standards and negotiate on your nonnegotiable you begin to sacrifice a piece of your dream. Some women believe it is more important to be in a relationship than to be in the relationship that they deserve. A successful relationship should meet your needs. If you need romance and affection you should be with someone who will provide that to you.

The hard part is differentiating between what you need and what you want. You do not throw a gift away just because you did not like the wrapping paper. This reminds me of this story I heard. There was an old man sitting on his porch while the rain was falling. It rained so much that the water came up to his porch. A rescue boat came and the rescuers told him "you cannot stay here, you should come with us." The old man said "God will save me." The people in the boat left. By now the water had reached the second floor. Another boat came by trying to rescue the man and again he declined. He told them just as he told the people in the first boat, "God will save me." An hour later the water had reached the third floor of the man's house. A third boat came by to help the man and for the third time he said, "God will save me." Shortly after this the man drowned. When he got to heaven he asked God, "Why didn't you save me?" God replied, "I sent three boats after you."

Sometimes we get so caught up in what things are supposed to look like that we miss the blessings that are right in front of our face. My point is not that you settle for the first man who shows interest in you. I want you to be open to love even if it does not look like what you thought it would. Know the difference between a man with a few flaws and a man with a deal breaker. Here are a few examples of possible deal breakers:

- He does not want children and all you have ever wanted was to be a mom.

- He does not get along with anyone in your family.

- He flirts with other women.

- He is possessive and overly jealous.

- He does not want to work.

- He is too much of a mama's boy.

- He has excessive baby-mama drama.

- He has a drinking or drug problem.

- He has been violent toward you.

- He cheats on you.

- He says he does not believe in marriage.

- He never admits to any wrongdoing or refuses to compromise.

- He never compliments you. In fact, he puts down your looks or your weight.

These examples are stark comparisons to flaws and imperfections. Take these "flaws" for example:

- You prefer a man to be over 6', but he is 5'9.

- He has a child already, but he maintains a healthy and platonic relationship with the child's mother, and he is an amazing dad.

- He may not be muscular, but when he gets dressed up he is so sexy.

- He may not have a degree, but he has his own business or a really good position at his job.

- He takes things a little slow, but he has begun integrating you into his life.

- He cannot afford to take you to the best restaurants in town, but he is creative and he always plans the most romantic dates.

If you are searching for the "perfect man" you will come up empty handed every time. What about finding a man that's perfect for you? We all have quirks, mannerisms and idiosyncrasies that make us unique. Whether it be good or bad you have to look at the man as a whole. To do that, you must be able to distinguish between life altering deal breaking issues and man that is not the personified image you've always imagined him to be.

Now that we have talked about him, let's talk about you. Being ready to date is about more than just being single. Here are 10 signs that you are ready to date:

1. You are confident in yourself and what you have to offer a man.

2. You are independent and fully capable of taking care of yourself.

3. You understand that every man you date will not necessarily be your husband.

4. You have identified your relationship nonnegotiable.

5. You have no residual bitterness or anger from failed relationships in your past.

6. You are not dating to validate your worth as a woman, but merely for companionship.

7. You are emotionally available.

8. You embrace your strengths and your weaknesses.

9. You approach new relationships with optimism.

10. You are willing to cut your losses and walk away if you are not getting what you need.

You are not truly ready to be in a relationship until you realize that you do not have to be. The key to enjoying your life is finding a way to enjoy it at every stage. Being single is not something you should be ashamed of. It should be something you celebrate and appreciate. You have the rest of your life to be a 'we' or an 'us.' Take the time to enjoy this 'me time.' There are perks to being single.

Utilize this free time to focus on developing your best self; mind, body, and spirit. Start working out, get a new hobby, go back to school, volunteer at a worthwhile charity, or travel the world. Cultivate and nurture relationships with your family and friends. Follow your own rules. If you want to spend next month's rent on a pair of red bottoms who is going to stop you – you have no one to answer to. Enjoy your life and tend to your relationship you have with yourself first.

THE DATING GAME

Sadly, some women do not feel whole unless they are someone else's other half. That's actually an oxymoron. There is such a thing as single and loving it. Do not get me wrong, being in a committed relationship with someone who loves and cherishes you is amazing, but there is so much to love about being single as well. Television shows like "Sex and the City" ruin it for all of us. Most likely you do not have a new love interest every week, and you and your girlfriends do not run around your city breaking hearts and dripping in Chanel. You may just spend your Saturday afternoons alone chilling in your pj's, with a mud mask on your face, eating cookie dough ice cream straight out of the carton while watching a *The Real Housewives of Atlanta* marathon. (That Nene is something else, isn't she?) Even if this is your life right now you can still be single and loving it. This is just a season and seasons change. Life is what you make it. It is all a matter of perspective.

CHAPTER 3
WHAT DOES YOUR BODY LANGUAGE SAY ABOUT YOU?

THE DATING GAME

Nonverbal communication is one of the most powerful tools we have. Whether you know it or not, you are constantly sending signals using body language. Let's imagine it is your very first date with a new guy. What are your eyes, shoulders, and posture saying? Here are a few example scenarios. You are at dinner with a friend and you see a couple at the next table. The man is looking sternly at the woman he is with and she has her shoulders slumped and is looking down while he is talking. Without even hearing what is being said, what can you infer from their body language? It is reasonable to suspect that the man is upset with the woman.

You spot another couple. The man has a big smile while he is talking. The woman he is with is smiling and leaning forward. They both erupt in laughter and she touches his hand. What can be inferred here? It is reasonable to assume that this couple is enjoying each other's company and that there is chemistry here. The good thing about body language is that you can practice exuding confidence until you really are confident. Let's talk about how you can use your body language to demonstrate confidence.

The key is to relax your entire body, especially your hands. Do not put them in your pocket, bite your nails, or fidget. Doing these things will completely give you away as being nervous. Sit or stand with your back straight, shoulders back, and smile. When you are interested in what someone is saying lean forward a little. Leaning back can send a message that you are uninterested, or in some cases even a bit standoffish.

Another thing you can do is to subtly mirror the actions of whoever is speaking. For example, if they are smiling while telling a story you should smile too. (Smiling is always very important. Confident people smile a lot because they believe they have nothing to worry about.) If you are on a date and you want to send a subtle sign of appreciation you could look them in the eyes, touch their hand and say, "I have had an amazing time with you tonight. Thank you." If you are not used to doing these things do not be overwhelmed; start small, but keep practicing until it comes as natural to you as breathing.

Men are not always the most upfront about how they are feeling. Men use approximately 13,000 fewers words than women according to a study conducted by University of Maryland School of Medicine and published in the Journal of Neuroscience. Researchers observed a group of 4 and 5 year olds. They discovered that girls have 30 percent more language protein in their brains than boys. Here is scientific proof that the saying "he is a man of few words" is true. This is why being able to read a man's body language is so important. Here are a few things to look for. A flirtatious smile is one of the most obvious signs of interest. He may take his gaze from your eyes to your mouth while you are talking. This could be an indication that he may want to kiss you. He raises his eyebrow ever so subtly when you are talking. You catch him stealing glances while you are not paying attention. he lick his lips, or guides you by gently placing his hand on your lower back. And there is my personal favorite: he watches you walk away.

Confidence is something that radiates from the inside out. The way you move and carry yourself tell so much more about you than words ever could. If utilized properly body language can help you send and decipher subtle messages sent to you from your date or anyone else for that matter. Whether you are attempting to confirm that your date is interested in you or you want the man staring at you at the end of the bar to get loss, you can do all of that and more by being able to properly use and read body language.

CHAPTER 4
WHAT DO YOUR CLOTHES SAY ABOUT YOU?

Have you ever heard the expression 'dress for the job you want'? You would be amazed to find out how much your outward appearance affects your inward one. In this chapter you will get a few tips on improving your self-esteem and confidence level. But first, let's start by dressing the part. Research has shown that women place emotions on clothing. We all have that dress in our closet that we get tons of compliments on and we know we look amazing in.

When you wear it you feel an instant confidence boost. We may also have that piece of clothing from a few years ago that we absolutely loved but no longer fits. Every time you see that item hanging in your wardrobe you frown and give off a heavy sigh. Let's face it, what you wear can alter your mood either positively or negatively. So, what do your clothes say about you? Clinical psychologist and author of the book *You Are What You Wear*, Dr. Jennifer Baumgartner, believes there is a 'psychology of dress.' (Baumgartner 2012). For example, does your wardrobe consist mostly of designer labels? There's nothing wrong with investing in quality pieces but is this masking a larger issue. Do you feel as though you will earn the respect of others if you have nice things? This could come across as trying too hard. Consider wearing more understated pieces and accent them with higher end accessories like a nice pair of shoes or handbag. You want people to appreciate you for who you are not who you wear. Here's another example, do you have a hard time getting rid of clothes that you either cannot fit, no longer your size or no longer suits your style? Is your wardrobe filled with clothing you never wear but you don't have the heart to throw them away? This could be a sign that a closet intervention is in order but it could also be a sign of clinginess. Do you also have a hard time getting rid of relationships that no longer fit? Maybe it's time to clean out your closet literally and metaphorically.

Men couldn't care less about what you wear; they are more interested in how you feel in what you are wearing. When you feel good about yourself you have a bit more of a sway in your walk. You sit up a little straighter. You look him right in the eyes. You are engaged, and he may find that engaging. It has been said that the sexiest thing a woman can wear is confidence. So let's dress for confidence.

When it comes to selecting the right clothing, it is all about dressing for your body type. The goal is to find the right pieces that flatter your particular body shape. We are not all 36-24-36 like the lyrics from the song "Brick House" by the Commodores. (Commodores 1977) Start by identifying your body type. Are you an hour glass, rectangle, apple, pear, or athletic build? Let's break this down a bit.

Hourglass Shape: Your weight is evenly proportioned. You are fuller in the hips and bust and much smaller in the waist. Clothing with a V-neck and items that accentuate your smaller waist look best on you. A line and body conscious skirts and dresses are also a good idea. If this is your body type wrap dresses should be your best friend.

Rectangle Shape: Your weight is also evenly distributed; however, you lack definition in the waist area. The key to dressing for this particular body type is creating the illusion of curves. Clothing with sweetheart neck lines and pieces that are belted at the waist are perfect for you. Ruffled tops and flirty skater style skirts are great for creating volume.

Apple Shape: You have a fuller figure. You have broader shoulders, fuller bust and mid-section but are smaller in the hips and thighs. Baby doll dresses and pieces with an empire waist are perfect for you. These types of pieces draw attention away from your midsection and accentuate your best features. Maxi dresses cinched in at the waist and strapless tops look amazing on you.

Pear Shape: You have a smaller bust and midsection but are fuller in the hips, thighs, and bottom. Clothing that fits and flares compliment your body shape best. Halter style shirts and dresses accentuate your petite figure. Tailored skirts are a great compliment to a fitted top.

Athletic Build: You have broader shoulders, and a smaller waist with toned and muscular legs. Creating curves is essential for this body type as well. Ruffles, peplum tops and fit-and-flare style dresses are perfect for you. Show off those amazing legs. Miniskirts and shorts will add a feminine edge to your style.

Add pieces to your wardrobe that suit your body type and flatter your figure. If you know you look amazing in wrap dresses because they accentuate your best features and make you feel sexy, buy them in several different styles, colors, and patterns. When you build your wardrobe with pieces that flatter you it builds your confidence. Building confidence when it comes to the way you look is important, because when you look good you feel good. Identify your flaws and insecurities, whether those flaws are about the way you look or the way you feel.

Focus on the positive and accentuate your best features and characteristics. It may help to write them down-both your flaws and your best features. Consider writing out a list of all of your flaws and shortcomings. Then turn your so-called flaws inside out. For example, 'I may have a small chest, but I have a butt you could bounce a quarter off of.' Or 'I may have been a teen mom but I still graduated high school on time and got my cosmetology license.' Establish a rebuttal in your mind for every negative thought.

Remind yourself of your attributes and accomplishments. Through all of the difficulties and adversities you have faced in life you have still accomplished so much. If necessary, write encouraging Post-it® Notes reminding yourself of how amazing you are and leave them everywhere; on your bathroom mirror, in your car, in your cubicle at work, and on your fridge. The more you see these notes the more you will begin to accept the messages. It may be necessary to reprogram your thought process.

Positive affirmations, like the ones you will use in these notes, are effective; however, they are often too vague. Be specific. Develop a mental picture of your life and begin to confess that. 'Say what you see until you see what you said' For example, 'I will marry a degreed professional who loves honors and cherishes me.' You are worth having an amazing partner who accepts you, flaws and all. Knowing your value is vital to the success of any relationship. There will be someone who finds your squeaky voice and high pitched laugh endearing. There will be a man willing to wait until marriage to be intimate with you. There will be a man willing to love your children like they were his very own. You have to drown out that voice in your head that will tell you, 'it is too late for you to get married,' 'who is going to want to raise another man's child,' or 'no man is going to want a woman with a past like yours.' Those are all lies. You must drown out the negative voices with louder affirmations of your worth and value.

Here is another tip; set a small but reachable goal for yourself and then achieve it. Action kills fear. Nothing does more for your confidence than a feeling of accomplishment. We are not necessarily talking about a monumental goal here. Start with a single step. You do not eat an entire steak in one bite, you break it up into smaller more manageable pieces.

Let's say you have taken an interest in that cute new guy who just started working in the finance department. Start with a smile and a friendly hello. Or maybe you would like to completely revamp your whole look. Start by adding a pop of color to your neutral wardrobe. If your goal is losing 30 pounds start by signing up for a weight loss program or getting a gym membership. No, you have not completed your goal already, but you are one step closer. Do not forget to give yourself credit for the progress you have made.

By giving yourself credit you are treating yourself well. People often treat us how we treat ourselves. If you are always putting yourself down and believe you do not deserve to be happy you will exude that. Sadly, the wrong man could take that lack of self-worth and exploit it. That is why healthy self-confidence is crucial in dating. *You teach people how to treat you.*

CHAPTER 5
IS HE INTO YOU?

THE DATING GAME

We have all been there. You start off taking an interest in a guy, and he treats you more like a friend than the object of his affection. You settle for this pseudo-best-friend role because it is your best chance to get close to him without showing your hand. How do you know if he is interested in you? Women are a bit more subtle in their mating dance than men. We stare into his eyes, laugh at his jokes, bat those Demi Wispies, and we throw in a playful touch here and there. (Keep it classy ladies; do not frisk him...yet).

Men can be a little harder to read. There is a difference between a man who merely wants to sleep with you and a man who wants to sleep with you AND get to know you. Make no mistake, he wants to sleep you. If he never thought about sleeping with you at some point he would not have asked you out. There are several reasons he has not made the first move. He could think you are out of his league. Some men are intimidated by beautiful women. The timing may not have been right.

We have all been out with our girls somewhere and some brave man walks up to the table and tries to talk to one of us. We cannot resist the urge to have a little fun at his expense. Some men would rather wait to catch you alone on the dance floor than risk being eaten alive by your barracudas – I mean friends. Fear of rejection is another reason. For whatever reason he has not made the first move. Be patient. The last thing you want to do is pursue him and appear desperate. In the bestselling book *He's Just Not That Into You* by Greg Behrendt and Liz Tuccillo here is what Behrendt had to say about women pursuing men.

Men, for the most part, like to pursue women. We like not knowing if we can catch you. We feel rewarded when we do. Especially when the chase is a long one. We know there was a sexual revolution. (We loved it.) We know women are capable of running governments, heading multinational corporations, and raising loving children — sometimes all at the same time. That, however, doesn't make men different. IT'S SO SIMPLE. Imagine right now that I'm leaping up and down and shaking my fist at the sky. I'm on my knees pleading with you. I'm saying this in a loud voice: "Please, if you can trust one thing I say in this book, let it be this: When it comes to men, deal with us as we are, not how you'd like us to be." I know it's an infuriating concept — that men like to chase and you have to let us chase you. I know. It's insulting. It's frustrating. It's unfortunately the truth. My belief is that if you have to be the aggressor, if you have to pursue, if you have to do the asking out, nine times out of ten, he's just not that into you. (And we want you to believe you're one of the nine, ladies!) I can't say it loud enough: You, the superfox reading this book, are worth asking out. (Behrendt and Tuccillo, 2004)

I agree with Behrendt wholeheartedly. Men thoroughly enjoy the thrill of the hunt. If a hunter wandered across a dead deer in the woods he would not think much of it. He did not kill it. He did not plan or strategize how he would hunt his prey. Playing hard-to-get is just as old a concept as dating itself, but it is necessary. In all actuality, the woman does the choosing – we just make the man think it was his idea in order to keep his ego intact. Ego aside, here are some signs that he may be into you:

- He makes concrete plans about future events with you. We are not talking about "one day I want you to meet my family" but "my parents are flying in this weekend and I would like you to meet them."

- He keeps his focus on you even when other women are around.

- What bothers you bothers him. If you are happy he is happy, and if you are sad he shares in that sadness, even though it does not affect him directly.

- He stakes his claim. He may not challenge other men to an arm wrestling contest, but he makes sure that other men know you are spoken for. He does this in a nonverbal way like putting his arm around you or holding your hand, perhaps. This is an example of a man's use of body language. Typically the touch is a little more familiar so as not to be confused with just being a friend. It may be a firm handshake or a head nod with a clenched jaw but you can tell he gets a little territorial when other men approach you.

- He is not afraid to be affectionate with you in public.

- If he is having a bad day he tells you that seeing you will make it better.

- He has given you a title. Typically there is a conversation and a mutual decision to become exclusive.

- He is not afraid of exclusivity. Commitment does not scare him. Once a man has found what he has been looking for, he is more than willing to take you off the market.

- He may become more serious about his finances. Some men start preparing financially when they are getting serious with a woman. He wants to make sure he can take care of you and a possible family

- He is uncomfortable taking money from you.

- When he talks about his future he is talking about you. He is not just saying "one day when I get married," he is saying "one day when we are married."

- He is willing to wait until you feel ready to be intimate. He is clearly attracted to you, but he is fine with just cuddling (for now).

- He spends quality time with you.

- He does not hold your past against you.

- He courts you. He may or may not have the means to wine and dine you often, but whatever he does have he is willing to share with you.

- He is upfront with you about his feelings. One of the biggest myths is that men do not talk about their feelings. That is not true. They may not do it as easily or as often a woman, but they are not afraid to be emotionally vulnerable when they feel safe. If he feels safe enough with you he will open up.

- He will show you he loves you with both his words and his actions. He may not be the type to write you poems but he may stop by your place with soup, cough medicine, Kleenex®, and a chick flick. He will take care of you when you are sick even though he would be missing the super bowl party his friends have been planning for weeks.

Unfortunately, there are men who prey on women's weaknesses and insecurities. If you are constantly bombarding him with your dream of the perfect wedding, the white picket fence, the 2.5 kids and a dog, he will play that role for you. Even if that is your ultimate goal for dating, be careful how much emphasis you put on it in front of a potential mate.

THE DATING GAME

Some men may use this information and exploit it as vulnerability. Guard your heart at first.

CHAPTER 6
THE ART OF FLIRTING

THE DATING GAME

Flirting is an art form. There is a right and wrong way to flirt. When a man does not know how to flirt he can come across as a creep or pervert. A woman who does not know can come across as easy or desperate. So, let's get down to the basics. The first step to flirting with someone new is to make sure they are available.

As old-fashioned as it sounds, it is still a good idea to check his ring finger. If he is wearing a ring it was not meant to be. Do not even waste your time getting to know him. It is my firm belief that the perfect man for you does not belong to someone else. If he fails to voluntarily let you know if he's attached you should ask. If he is not wearing a ring, then there is potential for something to happen. Eye contact is always a good idea. Women are a bit more subtle when we have seen someone who has caught our eye. We can look a man up, down, and sideways in a nanosecond. But men tend to take a bit more time, so most often you will catch him checking you out.

If he smiles be sure to sure to give him a warm and inviting smile back. If he is staring and making you feel like a piece of meat I recommend you pass. No woman wants to feel objectified or like she is being undressed with his eyes. Once he has smiled and you have smiled back, look away. There is nothing wrong with being a little coy and playing hard-to-get. If he is interested, most likely you will catch him staring again. For men, there is always the looming fear of rejection, so they are very careful when deciding whether or not to approach a woman.

The male ego can be quite fragile. There must be confirmation of mutual interest before they proceed. Men are always looking for a sign that their advances will be welcomed. If you continuously catch him checking you out he may be ready to make his move. Wait for him to introduce himself to you. If you are out with friends or at a club do not worry about missing an opportunity. If he is truly interested he *will* make contact with you before it is too late. He may be gathering the courage to approach you.

If you are shy do not worry; you can still master the art of flirting. You may have to rely more on some of the nonverbal communication skills we discussed earlier. Men do like shy women. It makes them feel special when they get you to open up. If he does strike up a conversation with you, keep things lively and light. Do not overshare and do not complain.

This is not the time to talk about past relationships, problems at work, financial issues, and so forth. Sharing too many personal details of your life too soon can be overwhelming and a turn off.

You may feel obligated to let him know what he is getting into in the interest of full disclosure, but oversharing can be a form of self-sabotage. Allow him to get to know you *gradually*. There should always be an air of mystery and intrigue about you. You can be an open book; just allow him to read one chapter at a time. Be honest. It is ok to say something like, "I heard the Patriots won the super bowl, but that is all I know about football. I would love it if someone was patient enough to actually teach me about the game." Be yourself. Do not waste your time trying to be who, or what, you think he wants you to be. If you do, you are not being true to yourself.

You want someone to want you for who you are, not who you are pretending to be. Do not, I repeat, *do not* bring up the topic of marriage. If it comes up somehow in conversation speak about it briefly then move one. Talking too much about marriage to a man you have just met could have him running for the hills. I know you have been subscribed to *Modern Bride* magazine for the past five years, and planning your wedding day since you were a little girl, but this is not the time to talk about that. Pay him a genuine compliment, like, "You are so easy to talk to." Complimenting his body this early on, though, may be a bit too forward and it may give off the wrong impression. Make sure that he sees you're interested but do it in the most subtle way possible.

THE DATING GAME

Imagine that you are at a restaurant and the guy at the table next to you has caught your eye. You could ask him a simple yet random question just to get his attention. "Excuse me do you know what time this place closes?" or, "May I borrow your salt." This engages the man without being too forward. This is one of the best ways to break the ice and start a conversation. Keep the interaction brief, but be warm and inviting.

If you are not sure what to talk about use your environment. Imagine this scenario: you are at one of those chain restaurants known for their buffalo wings. There is a big game on tonight and every man in the place has his eyes glued to the screen. While waiting for drinks at the bar you strike up a conversation with a really cute guy. You could say to him, "Wow, this place is packed tonight. Did you come here for the wings, the game, or both?" If he is receptive take this opportunity to fully engage him in conversation. Be sure to make your exit on a high note. You could say something along the lines of, "I'm having such a good time talking to you but I think I'm being a bad friend. I'm totally neglected my girlfriends and it's supposed to be girl's night out". You could also say, "You are so easy to talk to but I have an early morning meeting tomorrow so I have to go." The key is to be intriguing yet illusive. Always leave him wanting more. He may ask for your telephone number or ask you out to finish your conversation and find out more about you. The best flirts are amazing conversationalists. A man likes to feel as if it was his idea to approach you but in all actuality you lured him to you. From the first glance to the first conversation you were always in control. There is an art to flirting. When done properly it feels natural and organic but most importantly the man of interest never sees it coming.

,

CHAPTER 7
FIRST DATE DOS AND DON'TS

THE DATING GAME

Your flirting has landed you a first date with a new guy. The goal is to see if there is a connection, and find out if this is someone worth getting to know. Dating is a lot like an audition. You do not land every role you audition for. So do not take it personally if you do not get a call back. Dating is important for many reasons: companionship, learning more about the opposite sex, finding an appropriate candidate for marriage, and of course fun. Far too often we forget to just have fun. Every man you date will not necessarily be the man you marry and the father of your children. Do not start doodling your first name with his last name just yet. Before going out with someone new take the pressure off of yourself and the date: say to yourself, "My goal is to have fun and get to know a nice guy." Relax. If it does not work with this guy there will be another.

I am sure we have all heard the expression 'you never get a second chance to make a first impression.' Princeton psychologists Janine Willis and Alexander Todorov concluded from their research that all it takes is a tenth of a second to form an impression of a stranger from their face, and that longer exposures will not significantly alter those impressions. All you may have is a blink of an eye, so let's make it count. Always dress to impress. We addressed clothing earlier in this book but this is a little different. What you wear on the first date sends a message, and you want that message to be clear.

Find out what you will be doing or where you will be going on your date to ensure that you are dressed appropriately. You do not want to show up wearing a white figure-hugging body conscious dress if you will be going to a restaurant famous for their finger-licking -barbecue ribs. As tastefully as possible, play up your best features. There is a fine line between sexy and trashy, ladies. My mother always told me "what you may be willing to show you may be willing to share." You can be sexy and classy at the same time. That is not an oxymoron. The key is to leave something to the imagination. I know you want to show off 'the girls' with a deep plunging neckline, or wear a mini skirt to show off those amazing legs of yours, but do it in moderation.

It is perfectly acceptable to show a tasteful amount of cleavage as long as your cup doesn't runneth over so to speak. Don't wear the right thing the wrong way. Being overexposed can send the wrong message. There's a difference between a woman a man takes home and a woman a man takes home to meet his mother. Your attire could go a long way in helping him to determine what type of woman you are. Go for a sexy yet understated vibe. You don't need the attention of every man in the room you just want his.

Try a midi -skirt or a figure-flattering pair of skinny jeans. If you have amazing legs and want to show them off then cover up on top. Here's another tip; trends are great in general, but avoid them on your first date. Most men do not get (or fully appreciate) women's fashion. So save the harem pants, peplum tops, wedge sneakers, and so forth for girl's night out.

Also for a first date, avoid looking overly made up. If you are a makeup enthusiast that is fine, but keep things a bit more understated initially. Most men are not into heavy makeup, or so they think. In an article called, "Guys, do they really like us without makeup?" published in February 2012 edition of Cosmopolitan magazine, 68% of men said they preferred women wearing no makeup. However, when the same men were shown pictures of popular celebrities both with and without makeup 73% preferred the ladies wearing makeup. Research shows that a man's perception of what is natural and a woman's perception are completely different. Save the bold-cut crease with glitter liner, a fierce contour, and a bold lip for another night. Opt for a more subtle, natural-looking look.

Once you are looking great and are on that date, be sure to listen to your date. It's a good idea to interject something that they mentioned back into the conversation. I call it recycling. Take this example:

your date says, "I played football in my freshmen year of college before I got hurt and lost my scholarship. I still managed to finish school though. I must have had a hundred jobs to pay for school." You could say something like, "what kind of jobs did you have?" or "what did you major in." People love talking about themselves, especially when someone seems genuinely interested. Try not to dominate the conversation by talking about you. Think of it as a verbal tennis match. The conversation should go back and forth.

When you do talk, do not talk about your ex. The last thing you want to do is come across as bitter or still in love with an old flame. Also, never admit to still being in love with an ex. It only leaves your new date to wonder if they are supposed to be your rebound guy. No one wants to feel used. And if you speak too negatively about an ex you can come across as bitter. As you see, it is a lose/lose situation. If the topic is brought up say something like, "It just did not work out but I still wish him the best," or, "We were just going in different directions." Truthfully, if you are not completely over your ex you are not ready to date. The last thing you want to do is bring old baggage into a new relationship.

Another thing to avoid on a first date is oversharing. The basic rule for first-date conversations is 60/40. You should be listening sixty percent and talking forty. There is a fine line between giving your date enough information to determine if you two have things in common and telling him your entire life story before the check arrives. There should always be an air of mystery and intrigue about you. Do not forget: you should always leave him wanting more. Your date should not know every single thing about you after the first date. Be especially careful how much you divulge about your past relationships. The last thing you want to do is give a man you barely know the blueprint to your heart.

Keep in mind, this is someone you are getting to know, not someone you have known all of your life. He has no obligation to call you the next day or to continue getting to know you. Do not spend the entire date complaining about spending the last five years of your life with your no-good ex-boyfriend who refused to marry you after you had given him countless ultimatums. What you are really saying to this new guy is, 'you can take your time with committing to me. I have put up with that in the past.' Although you want to be comfortable, avoid being so comfortable that you say things like, "A year from now I'd like to be married," or, "Every man I have ever dated has cheated on me." This type of information could be used against you.

THE DATING GAME

Your date could quickly become Mr. Me Too. I am sure you have met someone like this before. For everything you say, he says, "oh yeah, me too." I want to get married, "me too." I want 3 children. "Me too." I hate infidelity in relationships, "me too." Everything should not be up for discussion on the first date. Allow him to earn your trust over the course of several dates before you begin sharing your deepest darkest secrets, fears, and insecurities.

Too much too soon could be overwhelming. If you have had a string of first dates that have never developed into anything more, you may want to ask yourself if you scared him away by revealing too much too soon. Before sharing something deeply personal or intimate about you ask yourself, "Why do I want to share?" If you can't determine a valid reason why he needs to know this, and know this now, then wait until he gets to know you better.

A woman who shares too much too soon is often needy. Don't be needy. The needy woman is the single man's nightmare. The book *Intimate Relationships* by Rowland S. Miller addresses the psychology of a needy women. According to the author there are four attachment styles. Of l the four attachment styles I am about to introduce this one most men would prefer.

THE DATING GAME

The first attachment style is the *assured girlfriend*. She knows what she has to offer in a relationship. She welcomes the idea of becoming close to someone and she does not have abandonment issues. She will encourage her man to go and hang out with the guys periodically. She would not text him the entire time or stay up all night worrying about him cheating on her with another woman. She's confident that what she gives her mate in their relationship is more than enough.

The second attachment style mentioned is the *needy girlfriend*. She is very unsure of herself and of her value. She fears that her man could leave her any minute. She constantly seeks validation, and often complains that she and her mate are not close enough. She is very insecure around other women. She may accuse her mate of cheating on her, or wanting to cheat on her, all the time.

The third attachment style is the *distant girlfriend*. She is strictly business. She has time for little things like closeness and intimacy. She is often a friend with benefits. She does not allow anyone to get close enough to hurt her, so she is very distant. It would take an extremely patient man who really loves her to get her to open up.

Finally, there is the *scared girlfriend*. Although she longs for closeness and intimacy, she is too afraid to make herself vulnerable enough to ask for it. She is not always open about her feelings but she is often jealous and suspicious of other women. Regardless of your attachment style, with the right partner and hard work you can overcome these issues. The key is to first identify your relationship weaknesses. Doctor Phil said it best: "You can't fix what you refuse to acknowledge."

This needy, distant, and scared behavior all stem from insecurities and a lack of self-esteem. Make sure that the effort you are putting into your relationship is reciprocated. You should not be the only one calling, texting, or making plans to see each other. If this is an area of weakness for you be sure to implement some of the confidence building strategies mentioned earlier in this book to help you with these issues. Then you can focus more on him, and figuring out if he is ready to take that next step. One of the most common mistakes made when entering or attempting to enter a relationship is the thought that someone will complete you. When Tom Cruise said "You complete me" to Renee Zellweger in the 1996 romantic comedy "Jerry Maguire" women all in theaters everywhere swooned. Romantic? Absolutely. Realistic. No. Your mate should compliment you not complete you. It is extremely unrealistic not to mention unfair to expect someone else to fill a void you have in yourself. Allowing someone to

completely you is giving them far too much power.
Never place yourself in such a vulnerable position
where your happiness is determined by someone else.

CHAPTER 8
WHEN WILL HE COMMIT?

THE DATING GAME

One of the biggest misconceptions when it comes to men is that they are not willing to commit. I am sure you have heard the expressions 'all men are dogs,' 'men only want one thing,' and 'men just want to sow their wild oats.' Yes, those are true for some men, but they most certainly are not true for all men. There comes a time in a man's life when he is ready, willing, and able to settle down. Men know that women have dreamed of our wedding days since we were little girls. The last thing they want to be is seat filler in their own life. They are leery of women who talk too much about marriage and children right away because they feel that you could just be using them to fill a void. If you are a woman whose biological clock is beginning to tick louder and louder and you have never been married a man could feel as if your interest in him is not genuine.

A man needs to feel like you are not afraid to walk away from him. There must be a real feeling that he could lose you. Loving a man unconditionally sounds incredibly romantic but it is not necessarily realistic. There should be conditions to your love. Love should be earned. You both should never stop doing the things you did to get each other. Your relationship should be one lifelong date. Never stop dating, not even after the 'I dos.'

THE DATING GAME

When a man feels like you complete him and make him better he is more likely to commit. You may have encouraged him to go back to school to pursue a dream of his that he thought was dead. Or maybe you encouraged him to stop renting his overpriced apartment and buy his first home. He will begin to picture his life being so much fuller and richer with you in it. When I met my husband he was a counselor at a summer camp making a little over minimum wage. He had obtained his Bachelor of Science degree but he lacked experience. I have never had a problem finding a job. In fact, interviewing was one of my specialties.

I taught a college course and I conducted mock interviews with my students, showing them the dos and don'ts for a successful interview. Together we worked on his resume and interview skills, and before we knew it he had landed his first position making more money than he had expected. I cannot take credit for that entirely. He had earned his degree, but he needed a little motivation and that is exactly what I gave him. When a man finds a woman who pushes him to reach new levels he is intrigued. It was my husband who pushed me to write this book, even when I insisted that I am a much better speaker than I am a writer. A successful relationship requires you to believe in the other person and his or her dreams.

THE DATING GAME

Once a man has worked to establish a life for himself and is in a good place financially, emotionally, and spiritually, he begins to seek out a wife. He looks for a compatible woman to be the mother of his children; a woman he can build a life with. Some men are very open and honest with their feelings and their intentions. They will tell you quite frankly that they are not interested in a committed relationship. Do not be naïve enough to believe that you can change his mind. As the late Maya Angelou says "when someone shows you who they are believe them." Take him at his word.

A man does not like when woman tries to change him. If you continue to pursue a meaningful lifelong relationship with a man who has already expressed to you that he does not want a commitment you are setting yourself up for heartbreak. Before you start wishing that men these days were more like the men of old, I do not think men have changed that much. Back in the day couples stayed together longer, yes, but it was not because the men cherished their women more or because men were more faithful. Now women are stronger, and more independent, and are no longer tolerating men who are not willing to be the faithful husbands we thought we married. Never mistake love for toleration.

THE DATING GAME

Just because a man stays with you does not mean he loves you. Men stay in relationships for any number of reasons; habit, financial stability, guilt, not having any place else to go, and trying to do the right thing (at least on the surface). Some women are often confused at how quickly a man they have been with for so long could quickly rebound, moving on to someone else in such a short period of time. When someone is not fully in love and committed to their partner they can easily detach themselves from one person and reattach themselves to someone else without the slightest hesitation. True love cannot be turned on and off like a switch; it takes time for love to grow and for love to fade away.

CHAPTER 9
LET'S TALK ABOUT SEX!

THE DATING GAME

I recently receive a letter from a woman who had sex with a man on the first date. She was surprised when he eventually started to treat her like a booty call. He never took her out on any dates, she had never been to his place, and he only called her late at night. Once you have sex with a man so early on in a relationship it is very difficult to start getting to know each other. Yes, you know each other intimately, but there was no connection built between the two of you. Be leery of relationships that are always on his terms but on your turf. Know the difference between what you are getting and what you deserve. Sleeping with a man on the first date is like getting your dessert before your dinner. After you have had dessert are you even still hungry?

Getting a man to sleep with you is far from challenging. Men see one night stands as a tremendous ego boost. Commonly referred to as *his terms her turfs*, these casual flings rarely end well because someone usually develops feelings for the other person. (Most likely like the woman in this scenario.) Men are wired completely different from women. It is much easier for them to emotionally detach themselves from sex.

Here are some signs that you may be a booty call or a casual fling:

THE DATING GAME

- You have never been (or have rarely been) to his place

- You have never been introduced to his friends or family.

- He is not an open book. There may be certain times of the day he has asked you not to call, or certain topics he will not discuss with you

- He never makes plans with you in advance or take you on dates.

- He calls, or returns your calls, late at night.

- You rarely see or hear from him during the daytime.

- He disappears periodically without a legitimate explanation.

- Every time you see each other you end up having sex.

- He says you two are just friends.

- He does not mind if you see other people.

- He does not acknowledge (or make any attempt to remember birthdays, Valentine's Day, or other holidays with you.

- He never posts any pictures with you on social media.

- He gives you no affection outside of the confines of the bedroom (no hugging, kissing or hand holding)

- He is not concerned about your problems.

- He does not integrate you into to his life in any way.

- He never spends the night.

- He says he does not "do relationships" yet he has had several girlfriends.

- He is in a relationship with someone else and he seems happy in pictures or on social media but the story he tells you is very different.

You can tell a lot about a man's true intentions towards you when you deny him sex. If he gives you attitude, becomes mean and distant and falls off the face of the Earth most likely it's because he just wanted sex. But if you deny him sex and he seems virtually un-phased and still interested in pursuing you and seeing where things go he may be genuinely interested in getting to know you on a deeper level. Only time will tell. Delaying intimacy is one of the biggest tools you have in obtaining a man's true intentions towards you.

By now you may have heard about the infamous 90 day rule. Some women swear by this like it's a scripture in the Bible. I promise you it's not. This rule states that you should get to know your partner at least 90 days before being intimate with him. The premise is that you will build a strong connection with your partner in the interim. Make no mistake, I'm not insinuating that the 90 day rule is preposterous. I just don't believe it should be taken so literally. The idea that you should get to know someone as well as possible before becoming intimate with them is sound advice. However, I don't believe he's a keeper just because he stuck around for 90 days without being intimate. What has he been doing in those 90 days? Has he been dating other woman and perhaps being intimate with them? Has he only seen you a few times in those 90 days or have you been together just about every day?

THE DATING GAME

Perhaps now you understand my reluctance to fully embrace such an idea. Don't get me wrong, you could discover after waiting 90 days that he's perfect...or patient. Some people find the idea of waiting, much less waiting until marriage to have to sex, to be old fashion, outdated and archaic. I will be honest with you, delaying intimacy is not a guarantee of a relationship's success, but neither is opting not to wait. As a Christian I must remind you that this is the way God intended it for a reason. 1 Corinthians 7:2 "But because of the temptation to sexual immorality, each man should have his own wife and each woman her own husband." In addition to this scripture there are countless others; 1 Thessalonians 4 3-5, 1 Corinthians 6-18, Hebrews 13:4 just to name a few. Imagine how much hurt and pain you could have avoided in your past relationships had you delayed sex and gotten to know him a bit better. Anyone can pretend to be your prince charming for a few days, weeks or even months. Abstaining from premarital sex is not only pleasing to God, you are also allowing your potential mate enough time for his true colors to emerge. A man who is not genuine and authentic will eventually get tired of pretending to be someone he's not. God's request that you refrain from premarital sex was not to ruin your good time, it was designed this way to protect your heart. "Above all else, *guard your heart*, for everything you do flows from it" Proverbs 4:23. Even those of you who have already be sexually active can still make the choice to abstain until such time as you are married or at the very least until you've determined your love interests intentions. I know what you're thinking, "who does that these days?" Honestly, very few people. If you are waiting until you are married you are in the minority. However, there are proven scientific studies that show that delaying intimacy leads to a more fulfilling sex life and a more stable relationship. In the Journal of Family Psychology's study called "Relate" 2,035 couples who delayed sex until they were married were surveyed. In comparison to couples that did not wait these couples rated the quality of their sex lives 15% high than their counterparts. Twenty two percent rated the relationship stability higher, and they rated twenty percent higher in relationship satisfaction.

I've received countless letters in the past from women who thought they could engage in casual sex and not get emotionally attached. In nine out of ten of those cases the woman developed feelings for her partner. Never mistake a man who is simply grateful that you are being intimate with him without any type of commitment nor effort on his part as love. Men appreciate and respect women with standards. He may carry on a sexual relationship with you for years and never develop actual feelings for you. What you need to understand is that men are wired completely different from women. It is much easier for them to emotionally detach themselves from sex. Don't assume that because he's sleeping you or being nice that he loves you, cares for you or even developing feelings for you. Unlike women, men can't get sex whenever they want so when the opportunity presents itself they take advantage. A man loves a challenge. If he does not find you challenging he will not make the effort. Make yourself a challenge. Don't just play hard to get *be* hard to get.

THE DATING GAME

CLOSING

THE DATING GAME

As humans we all have basic needs: food, water, shelter, and, for the vast majority of us, love. That need to be loved sometimes drives us to partake in and pursue relationships that are unfulfilling. I love the saying, "Follow your heart but take your brain with you." You should approach each relationship with optimism but the relationship must also make sense. We are all looking for the secret to finding love.

Some of you have read this entire book waiting for the moment I am about to share with you. Are you ready? Love finds you. When you are so desperate to find love you often find infatuation. Infatuation is a lot like fool's gold. It looks like the real thing but in all actuality it has no value. You have to love yourself before you can love anyone else because you are what you attract. If you have been attracting the same type of guy you have to realize that it is something about you that is attracting this type of behavior. It may be time to take a hard and introspective look at yourself. If you keep dating users who want you to pay for all of your dates, ask you to borrow money which they never pay back, or who move in with you but don't help pay any of the bills, you will have to change your behavior in order to attract something different. The definition of insanity is doing the same thing over and over and expecting a different result.

Maybe you have noticed that I have spent quite a large portion of this book focusing on confidence. That's largely because a man will treat you like you treat yourself. If you carry yourself like a lady worthy of his best, his best is exactly what he will offer you. That is exactly why setting standards and having a list of 'must haves' is so important. As a woman you must realize how powerful you are. You are in control of your own love life. If you don't feel loved, appreciated, respected or cherished you can make another choice.

Regardless of your age or stage you are in your life you do not have to settle. Never forget the power of choice and the freedom that comes with it. My hope is that you walk away from this book with a strong sense of empowerment. Embrace the single life and you enjoy it. You will be amazed by the types of men that approach you when you know who you are and exactly what you want. There is no need to throw a pity party because all of your friends are married with children and you are not: you are just as smart, just as attractive, and just as likeable as they are.

A woman in a relationship is no better than you are, regardless of what your peers, parents, friends, or society may tell you. Being in a relationship does not define who you are. You are much more than who you date. There is someone out there for all of us and there is definitely someone out there for you. You are someone's answered prayer. Your time will come and you will be ready. But until then, take this time to go on a journey of self-discovery. Date yourself. Fall in love with the person you see in the mirror. Why not find yourself, and let love find you?

THE DATING GAME

BIBLIOGRAPHY

THE DATING GAME

Baumgartner, Jennifer J. *You are what you wear: what your clothes reveal about you.* Boston: Da Capo Press, 2012.

Behrendt, Greg. *He's Just Not Into You: The No Excuses Truth To Understanding Guys.* New York: Simon Spotlight Entertainment, 2004.

"Brick House." The Commodores. Commodores. Motown. 1977.
"Guys, do you really like us without makeup?" *Cosmopolitan*, February 2012. cosmopolitan.com.

Jeffers, Susan J. *Feel the fear and do it anyway.* San Diego: Harcourt Brace Jovanovich, 1987.

Love Jones. DVD. Directed by Theodore Witcher. United States: New Line Home Video, 1999.

Miller, Rowland. Intimate Relationships. 6th ed. Columbus, OH: McGraw-Hill, 2011.

Sex and the City. HBO. 1998. Television.

THE REAL HOUSEWIVES OF ATLANTA. BRAVO. 2008. ATLANTA. TELEVISION.

Departments of 1Physiology and 2Psychiatry, and 3Department of Pharmacology and Program in

THE DATING GAME

Neuroscience, University of Maryland School of Medicine,

The Journal of Neuroscience, February 20, 2013 • Vol. 33, Issue 8:pages 3276 −3283

DOI:10.1523/JNEUROSCI.0425-12.2013

THE DATING GAME

CPSIA information can be obtained at www.ICGtesting.com
Printed in the USA
LVOW01s1332240315

431808LV00023B/371/P